INVESTIGATING
TOMBS & MUMMIES

EXCAVATION
EXPLORATION

JESSIE ALKIRE

Checkerboard Library

An Imprint of Abdo Publishing
abdopublishing.com

abdopublishing.com

Published by Abdo Publishing, a division of ABDO, PO Box 398166, Minneapolis, Minnesota 55439. Copyright © 2019 by Abdo Consulting Group, Inc. International copyrights reserved in all countries. No part of this book may be reproduced in any form without written permission from the publisher. Checkerboard Library™ is a trademark and logo of Abdo Publishing.

Printed in the United States of America, North Mankato, Minnesota
052018
092018

Design: Sarah DeYoung, Mighty Media, Inc.
Production: Mighty Media, Inc.
Editor: Megan Borgert-Spaniol
Design elements: Mighty Media, Inc., Shutterstock, Spoon Graphics
Cover photographs: iStockphoto, Shutterstock, Spoon Graphics, Wikimedia Commons
Interior photographs: Alamy, pp. 8 (top), 11; AP Images, pp. 9 (bottom), 23, 25, 27, 29; iStockphoto, p. 5 (left, top right); Shutterstock, pp. 4, 5 (middle right, bottom right), 7, 13, 17 (bottom left); Wikimedia Commons, pp. 8 (bottom), 9 (top), 17 (top left, right), 19, 21

Library of Congress Control Number: 2017961581

Publisher's Cataloging-in-Publication Data
Names: Alkire, Jessie, author.
Title: Investigating tombs & mummies / by Jessie Alkire.
Description: Minneapolis, Minnesota : Abdo Publishing, 2019. l Series: Excavation
     exploration l Includes online resources and index.
Identifiers: ISBN 9781532115264 (lib.bdg.) l ISBN 9781532155987 (ebook)
Subjects: LCSH: Mummies--Juvenile literature. l Tombs--Juvenile literature. l Discovery
     and exploration--Juvenile literature. l Excavations (Archaeology)--Juvenile literature.
Classification: DDC 932--dc23

CONTENTS

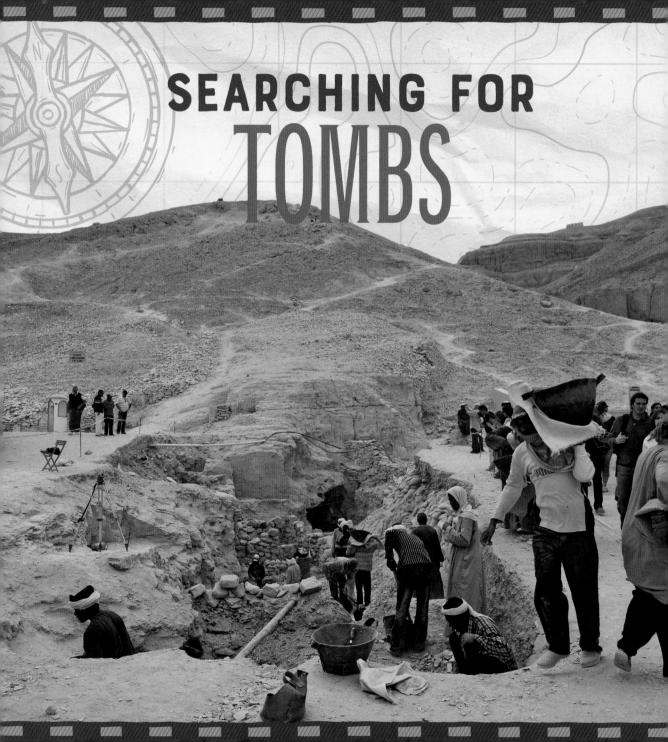

SEARCHING FOR
TOMBS

THE EGYPTIAN SUN BEATS ON YOUR BACK AS YOU DIG IN THE SAND.

You feel like you're covered in sand and might never be able to wash it away. This thrills you! You feel like you belong here, in the Valley of the Kings.

You're surrounded by a crew of other archaeologists and volunteers. But you're the leader of this expedition. You've found gold pieces and jewelry scattered in the earth over the past weeks. Your goal is to find the lost tomb of a king!

You press your shovel into the earth with all your weight. Crack! There's solid stone behind the crumbling dirt. You take your **chisel** and chip away as quickly as you can. A hole forms in the stone. You keep chiseling until the hole is large enough to look through.

You turn on a flashlight and peer through the hole. All you see are glittering jewels and gold. You've achieved your goal. You've found a spectacular tomb in the Valley of the Kings!

WHAT ARE
TOMBS & MUMMIES?

In many prehistoric **cultures**, the dead were laid to rest in their own homes. By ancient times, the dead were buried in separate chambers or vaults called tombs. The purpose of tombs was to provide shelter and protection for the dead.

Many tombs were simple stone structures. But some ancient civilizations buried their dead in elaborate tombs, such as pyramids. These tombs also served as memorials for people to enjoy.

Tombs can teach archaeologists much about the civilizations that built them. So can the bodies buried within tombs. Many ancient civilizations mummified bodies before placing them in tombs.

Mummification usually involved removing organs, applying chemicals, and wrapping the bodies in cloth. This kept the bodies from decaying. Mummification was often based on the belief that bodies needed to be preserved for their spirits to live on.

Certain cultures created tombs and mummies through the **Middle Ages**. Since then, people have more commonly been

Many tombs housed items such as food and personal possessions. It was thought that these objects would accompany the dead to the afterlife.

cremated or buried in **cemeteries**. Today, tombs and mummies help archaeologists learn how ancient **cultures** lived and thought about death.

TIMELINE

5000 BCE

The Chinchorro people of South America create mummies to remember the dead.

1917

German archaeologist Max Uhle excavates the first Chinchorro mummies.

2500s BCE

Egyptians build the Pyramids of Giza to house the bodies of kings.

1922

Howard Carter excavates the tomb of King Tut. He finds Tut's mummy the next year.

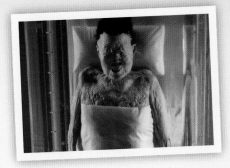

1972

Workers discover Lady Dai's mummy in China.

2008

Scientists collect **DNA** from King Tut's bones.

1991

Hikers find a frozen mummy in the mountains between Italy and Austria. It is later named "Ötzi the Iceman."

2015

Radar scans show evidence of secret chambers in King Tut's tomb.

CHAPTER 2

THE FIRST
MUMMIES

The oldest mummies ever found were created around 5000 BCE in Peru and Chile. A group called the Chinchorro lived in these areas during this time. The first Chinchorro mummies were found in 1917. German archaeologist Max Uhle was excavating a site near Arica, Chile. He uncovered several mummies from the site.

Uhle studied the mummies to understand how they were created. The Chinchorro first removed the skin, limbs, and organs of dead bodies. Then they filled the bodies with straw or grass. The bodies were also covered in a paste made from ash. The paste hardened, and the body was reassembled and painted black or red.

Since Uhle's discovery, hundreds of Chinchorro mummies have been found in Peru and Chile. Most Chinchorro mummies were discovered when a water company dug a new water line in Chile in 1983. Archaeologists recovered 96 mummies there!

These mummies have taught archaeologists much about how the Chinchorro people mourned the dead. The mummies were decorated and repainted over time. In some cases, the mummies' feet looked worn, as if they had been standing upright. Archaeologists think the mummies were kept in homes or as statues before later being buried. This was likely a way to honor and remember the dead.

In some ancient societies, it was mostly royalty and the wealthy who were mummified. But the Chinchorro mummified people of all classes.

EGYPTIAN TOMBS

While the Chinchorro produced the first known mummies, the most famous mummies come from Egypt. There, many dead bodies were naturally mummified in the region's dry sand and heat. Egyptians likely discovered these natural mummies and decided to create artificial mummies. They did so around 2600 BCE. These Egyptian mummies were kept in tombs.

The most famous Egyptian tombs are the Pyramids of Giza. These were built around the 2500s BCE. But, they were plundered by robbers for centuries. Many **artifacts** from the tombs were lost.

Other Egyptian burial sites were more concealed than the Pyramids of Giza. The Valley

DIG THIS!

To create artificial mummies, Egyptians removed the organs from dead bodies. Then they dried the bodies with salts and wrapped them in layers of linen.

of the Kings is a region famous for its tombs. Unlike the Pyramids, these tombs are underground.

The Valley of the Kings housed tombs beginning in the 1500s BCE. The tombs had stairs that led to multiple chambers. The chambers housed mummies along with food, wine, and riches for the afterlife.

The three Pyramids of Giza were built for Egyptian kings Khufu, Khafre, and Menkaure. It was believed these kings would become gods in the afterlife.

KING TUT

Despite their underground location, tombs in the Valley of the Kings were also plundered by robbers. Formal excavations began in the 1800s. Many excavators were only interested in finding treasures and **artifacts** to bring back to Europe. Excavations became more focused in the late 1800s as standard **techniques** were developed.

By the early 1900s, nearly every tomb in the Valley of the Kings had been plundered or excavated. But the tomb belonging to King Tutankhamun, or King Tut, was yet to be discovered. British archaeologist Howard Carter was determined to find Tut's tomb. He began his search for the lost king in 1914.

On November 4, 1922, a boy assisting Carter discovered a stone step. For weeks, Carter and his crew uncovered more steps that led to a sealed door. Carter **chiseled** through the door. Inside, he discovered a chamber full of gold and riches!

KING TUT'S TOMB CHAMBERS

The chambers of Tut's tomb held thousands of **artifacts**.
Among them were **chariots** and model boats.

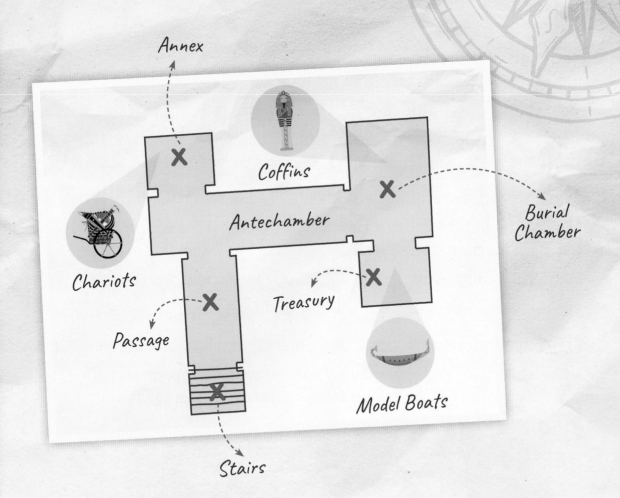

Annex

Coffins

Chariots

Antechamber

Burial
Chamber

Passage

Treasury

Stairs

Model Boats

Over the following weeks, Carter excavated the antechamber of Tut's tomb. This was the outer chamber that led to Tut's burial chamber. On February 16, 1923, Carter opened the burial chamber, which housed Tut's **sarcophagus**.

Inside the stone sarcophagus were three nested **coffins**. The innermost coffin contained Tut's mummy. Carter tried to remove the mummy from the coffin, but the mummy was stuck inside.

So, Carter used a **chisel** to cut Tut's remains from the coffin. He also cut off the mummy's head and limbs to separate it from its gold ornaments. Then, Carter reassembled Tut's remains and placed them in a wooden box filled with sand. The mummy was studied and later put on display in its tomb in the Valley of the Kings. It remains protected there today.

Experts have criticized Carter's handling of Tut's mummy. Archaeologists have since learned to better preserve their findings for future study. But Carter also set good examples in his careful study of Tut's tomb. He photographed and sketched thousands of items found inside the tomb's chambers. These **artifacts** have helped advance researchers' understanding of Egyptian **culture** and King Tut's life.

HOWARD CARTER

Howard Carter was a British archaeologist and ancient-Egypt scholar born in 1874. At 17 years old, he moved to Egypt to work on excavation sites. His job was to sketch **artifacts** that archaeologists found. Carter began to oversee excavations in the 1900s.

In 1922, Carter discovered King Tut's tomb. He found Tut's mummy the next year. Carter continued to oversee the tomb's excavation for ten years. He later published a book about his finds.

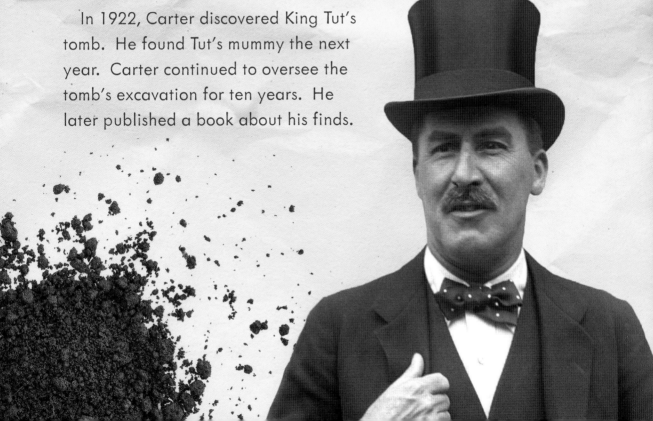

LADY DAI

While Egyptian mummies are the most famous, some of the best-preserved mummies come from China. China's most famous mummy is of Lady Dai, a noblewoman in ancient China. Her real name was Xin Zhui. She likely died around 160 BCE at about the age of 50.

Lady Dai was discovered in 1972. The previous year, workers had been digging a bomb shelter in a hill near Changsha, China. As they dug, they noticed strange things. The soil began to crumble, and it was giving off flammable gas.

Officials sent a team of archaeologists to search the area. The archaeologists knew that decaying bodies sometimes released flammable gases. After weeks of digging, they discovered an underground tomb. Inside, they found thousands of **artifacts** and the outer **coffin** containing Lady Dai.

Lady Dai's mummy was found inside four nested coffins. The body was wrapped in many layers of silk. The inner coffin also had a mysterious liquid inside. Researchers think the liquid may have had preservation properties, but they are not certain.

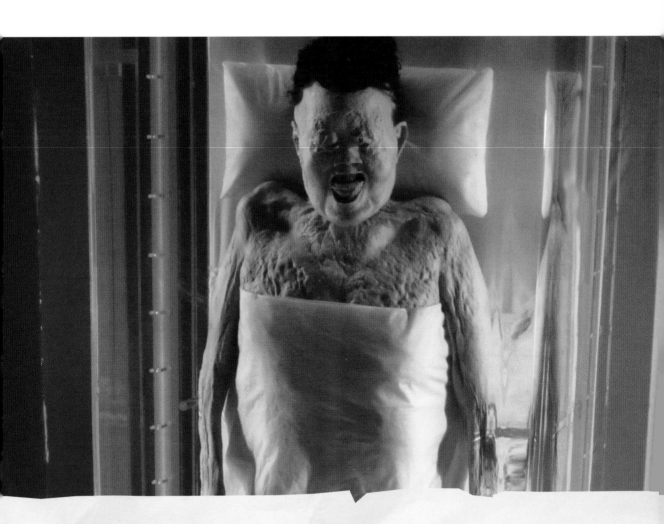

Lady Dai's tomb was sealed with clay and a carbon material called charcoal. This prevented any bacteria or liquid from getting into or out of the tomb.

Lady Dai is one of the best-preserved mummies in history. When archaeologists found her body, the skin was soft and the joints could bend. The body even had hair on the head and blood in the veins!

Doctors performed a thorough examination of Lady Dai. They found all her organs in place. The doctors determined she had lived with several medical conditions, including high blood pressure and liver disease. They also discovered blood clots, which indicated Lady Dai had died of a heart attack.

Researchers also carefully studied the **artifacts** found in Lady Dai's tomb. The tomb contained clothing, wooden carvings, food, and more. These items helped archaeologists understand how ancient Chinese royalty lived.

The tomb also showed how this **culture** viewed death. Like the Egyptians, the ancient Chinese expected to live on in the afterlife. Elaborate burials, like Lady Dai's, were ways to prepare for this. Today,

DIG THIS!

Lady Dai's body was so well preserved that researchers knew what she had eaten before her death. Doctors examining her mummy found more than a hundred melon seeds in its stomach and intestines!

China's Hunan Provincial Museum houses the mummy of Lady Dai along with an artistic recreation of the noblewoman.

scientists are still studying Lady Dai to find out how she is so remarkably preserved.

FROZEN IN TIME

While many famous mummies were artificially created, many others were naturally made. Some of these mummies were created in extreme cold. Their bodies were frozen and preserved.

Ötzi the Iceman is one of the most famous natural mummies. In 1991, tourists were hiking along the snowy mountain border between Italy and Austria. During their journey, they came upon the upper half of a man's body sticking out of ice.

Police thought the body was recently dead. But rescuers were unable to free the body from the ice. It took ice picks to finally do so.

Officials brought in Austrian archaeologist Konrad Spindler to examine the mummy. He estimated it was at least 4,000

DIG THIS!

Ötzi was named by a journalist after the Ötztal Alps, the location of the mummy's discovery site.

A model of Ötzi the Iceman is on display in the South Tyrol Museum of Archaeology in Bolzano, Italy. It shows what Ötzi might have looked like when he was alive.

years old! Scientists have since used more precise dating methods to determine Ötzi's age. They revealed that Ötzi lived more than 5,300 years ago. This makes his body one of the oldest mummies ever found!

MUMMY
TECHNOLOGY

Archaeologists now have many advanced **technologies** to study mummies. Imaging tools create detailed images of a mummy's body. These images can show scientists what a mummy's bones and organs look like. They can even determine a cause of death!

Scientists have used these tools to study Ötzi the Iceman. In 2001, researchers used **X-rays** and **CT scans** to look inside the mummy's body. The resulting images revealed an arrowhead in Ötzi's shoulder.

Researchers believed the arrow had cut a blood vessel and caused Ötzi to bleed to death. Scientists later used CT scans of the mummy to suggest Ötzi died from a blow to the head. Whatever the exact cause of death, scientists agree that Ötzi was murdered.

Researchers have also used advanced **techniques** to better understand Ötzi's life. In 2010, scientists collected **DNA** from the mummy's **pelvic** bone. By studying the DNA, scientists determined Ötzi's blood type, diseases, and even what foods he may have eaten!

Ötzi is preserved in a refrigerated cell at the South Tyrol Museum of Archaeology. The cell recreates the cold conditions in which the mummy was found.

Scientists have also used recent **technologies** to study mummies that were found long ago. One example is King Tut. The cause of Tut's death has long been a mystery. In 2008, researchers studied Tut's **DNA** to try to find answers.

Scientists collected the DNA from Tut's bones. They also tested the DNA of Tut's close relatives. The researchers determined that Tut's mother and father were related. This was common in Egypt at this time. But it often resulted in health issues for the children. Tut's DNA also revealed that he had a blood disease called malaria.

Researchers examined Tut's body using **CT scans**. They found that he had a deformed foot and broken leg. The malaria would have weakened Tut's health and prevented his injuries from healing. Some experts think a combination of these factors may have caused Tut's death.

However, not all researchers trust the results of DNA testing on Tut's mummy. They point out that Carter's handling of the mummy decades ago may have

DIG THIS!

Egyptian mummies were usually buried with their hearts still in their bodies. But King Tut's heart has never been found.

caused **contamination**. Scientists hope advances in **DNA** testing will provide more reliable information about those who were preserved as mummies.

In 2007, archaeologists opened King Tut's sarcophagus. They later moved the mummy to a climate-controlled case for public viewing.

UNDERSTANDING
THE PAST

Today's archaeology concentrates on understanding the past. Scientists want to learn more about ancient humans and teach the public as well. Tombs and mummies are important for this work.

One way archaeologists learn and teach others about the past is through imaging tools such as **CT scans** and **3-D** printing. Archaeologists use CT scans to see inside tombs and mummies. This creates highly detailed images. Then, 3-D printers turn these images into **replicas** of tombs and mummies. Some replicas are even made to show what a mummified body looked like when it was alive.

These methods have been used to make replicas of King Tut, Ötzi the Iceman, and other mummies. The original mummies and tombs remain protected. Meanwhile, people can observe and learn from the replicas.

Archaeologists have made great progress in excavating and studying tombs and mummies. But many mysteries still remain.

A Swedish research institute has developed a system that allows people to interact with scans of mummies. The scans were created using 3-D imaging technologies.

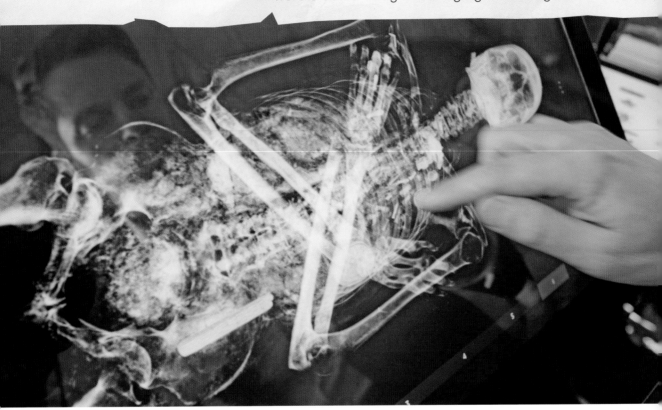

In 2015, archaeologists used radar scans to look inside King Tut's tomb. They think there are secret chambers yet to be discovered. Tombs and mummies will be providing clues about human history for many years to come!

GLOSSARY

artifact — an object made by humans long ago for a practical purpose.

cemetery — a place where dead people or pets are buried.

chariot — a two-wheeled horse-drawn carriage commonly used in ancient battles.

chisel — a tool with a flat, sharp end that is used to cut and shape a solid material such as stone, wood, or metal.

coffin — a box or a chest for burying a dead body.

contamination — the process of contaminating, or making unfit for use by adding something harmful or unpleasant.

CT scan — a 3-D image of an object's structure created by a combination of X-ray images.

culture — the customs, arts, and tools of a nation or a people at a certain time.

DNA — a material in the body that helps determine what features a living thing will inherit. "DNA" stands for *deoxyribonucleic acid*.

Middle Ages — a period in European history that lasted from about 500 CE to about 1500 CE.

pelvic — relating to the pelvis. The pelvis is the wide, curved bone structure between the legs and spine of a skeleton.

replica — an exact copy.

sarcophagus — a stone coffin, especially one that has been decorated with a sculpture or engraving.

technique (tehk-NEEK) — a method or style in which something is done.

technology (tehk-NAH-luh-jee) — a machine or piece of equipment created using science and engineering, and made to do certain tasks.

3-D — having length, width, and height. "3-D" stands for *three-dimensional*.

X-ray — an invisible and powerful light wave that can pass through solid objects.

ONLINE RESOURCES

Booklinks
NONFICTION
NETWORK
FREE! ONLINE NONFICTION RESOURCES

To learn more about tombs and mummies, visit **abdobooklinks.com**. These links are routinely monitored and updated to provide the most current information available.

INDEX